SIMPLE WAYS TO STEP OUTSIDE OF YOUR COMFORT ZONE

7 Day Program

Letting go of an outdated life

Sonia Barrett

TIMELINE PUBLISHING INC.
North Hollywood CA,

Timeline Publishing
& Media Relations Inc
We spread The Word

Simple Ways to Step Outside of Your Comfort Zone
7 Day Program
Copyright © 2017 by Sonia Barrett

Cover Art by Lillian Fidler Designs
Published by
Timeline Publishing & Media Relations Inc.,

Timeline Publishing & Media Relations Inc.,
12439 Magnolia Blvd, # 199,
North Hollywood, CA 91607

To inquire about special discount rates on bulk purchases, please contact
Timeline Publishing & Media Relations Inc.,
818-899-1133
info@timelinepublishinginc.com
Timeline Publishing & Media Relations Inc.,
12439 Magnolia Blvd. Suite 199
North Hollywood, CA 91607

Email: **info@timelinepublishinginc.com**
Website: **wwwtherealsoniabarrett.com**
ISBN 978-0-9913457-8-6
Library of Congress Control Number
2017907697

Contents

Simple ways to step outside of your comfort zone

Simple ways to step outside of your comfort zone

Transform!

INTRODUCTION

PROFOUND POWER IN LEAVING YOUR COMFORT ZONE

Leaving your comfort zone requires an observation of the way that you think, what you believe, what you tell yourself followed by an acknowledgment of the choices you've made. This involves an honest introspective of your life.

This handbook compels you to notice your comfort zones even when it is believed that there are none. Being stuck in certain comfort zones can indeed affect even the way that we age. It is essential that these bodies are fed new experiences. Cells are sustained by the energy of an expansive mind. These new experiences create new neural pathways in the brain. Your brain and your body receive a message of aliveness! That message says that I am not done with life and that I have no expiration date!

The impediment is that most often we don't think deeply enough and so the realization of a comfort zone is easily dismissed as being insignificant, yet it has everything to do with the progression of ones journey. You are a traveler, an astronaut here to maximize the human experience. We are here to process sensations in these bodies, the sensation of emotions and feelings. Living a safe life becomes

2

nothing more than a predictable life. We are addicted to the predictability of our lives. Such predictability forms patterns which serve as a blueprint from which one's life functions. The unknown holds the magic! Leaving our comfort zone transports us to an unlimited life!

The question that we should ask our self from time to time is "am I too comfortable in my predictable life?" How often do we embark on this self-examination. After reentering the corporate world in 2000 (after many years of being self-employed) I knew that my re-entrance represented much more than the pleasure of receiving a paycheck. I realized that my return would present me with opportunities for inner growth. I would discover things about myself as well as to incorporate a certain level of discipline and order, tools that would become essential in the not so distant future. I had no knowledge of what that future would hold. Somehow I was aware that once I had exhausted my reasons for being there the urge to move forward would arise and I would begin to feel a nudge.

It is important to be reminded of the nature of reality as collectively experienced and its influence on the way that we view ourselves. The endless need to give ones power away to various people and systems has served to keep many

3

disempowered. This level of disempowerment has become a natural way of life, making it a bit more challenging to be detected. It is important to now be aware of our investment in the experience. We can then determine if and when we have had our fill.

Charting a new course is about self-reliance. Despite the apparent surrender of our will, we have always been in charge of our journey. It seems to be part of the human program to surrender to any perceived "higher power" be it human or of alien origin (not of this world), someone to "save" us. Nonetheless we have selected what truths we choose to hide from ourselves. We decide to what degree we will "live" the illusion of relying on external conditions to dictate our lives. To be part of this reality is complex, simple and confusing. It's an endless paradox Why is that? Being a human being requires a commitment in order to be fully invested in the experience; an experience layered with emotional variety.

Choices and emotions change in an instant like the dream world as scenes morph one into another. When we awake from our dream state we remember the shifting scenes and people changing from one to the next in the midst of a scene. While we are dreaming however these occurrences are generally not realized as being out of order, so there is no concern for these automatic and fluid changes. So it is in our waking (dream) experience we don't notice much of the changes that are happening while we are in the midst of our moment to moment lives because we are fully invested in the stories being played out. However should we choose to be more present and less automated we will then notice these occurrences. This kind of awakening stirs a shift in the choices we begin to make.

There are endless choice points in this ocean of possibilities, each choice point opens up a portal aligned with a particular series of experiences, we are then off and running; not being the wiser that we are the influencer of the series of experiences to follow. These experiences include all of our interactions with people, places and things soon to be experienced. Much like the influencers of social media attracting thousands of followers, these influencers become a power-full point from which strong and expanding branches emerge; a chain of minds linked to a particular field of information/data. As individuals we are the influencers of our reality and all that is linked to it.

Life branches off from you! It's time to redefine your reality, as your current reality "relies" on the power you supply to it. It has always been that way.

To be in a space of self-empowerment is to be empowered or to be reminded of your power. Self-empowerment is about awakening to the realization of the degree to which power is being generated by you in every moment. It is this power that supports your reality; you are the generator of the charge being supplied to your personal world. Every cell in our body experiences the waning and the waxing of this power. Most often we struggle with defeat. These moments of defeat (as perceived) are the moments when we step away from the awareness of self-empowerment. We then expel a tremendous amount of power to hold that feeling and belief in place, even then we are powerful as we have the ability to convince ourselves that we are not. These are the experiences that support our surrender to these comfort zones we find ourselves in. We seek a safe haven. Because of the hypnosis and addiction to the external world our sense of self-empowerment fluctuates according to the stimuli delivered to evoke various emotional responses.

To be resilient is to step into your power and to own it unapologetically! Resilience is about pliability. It is about creating new neural pathways. It is about stepping up to authentic ideas and being creative in charting a new course despite the projected expression of the external world. Our relationship with the external world is completely dependent on one's perception and on one's current design and rules for your personal reality. You are the ultimate influencer although influenced by subconscious programs which stem from external influences. It all drives us to scratch our head in confusion. However the key to this hodgepodge is to awaken to your-self. Self-awareness is about stepping up to the awareness of this hodgepodge function of this reality experience; the dreamscape paradox.

See this as an opportunity to take charge of one's reality and to explore that new business you have been pondering or perhaps walking away from your job or ongoing health issues (what is the payoff for your chronic health condition) or relationships that no longer serve you or perhaps reinterpreting your perception of your current work environment or relationships. Sometimes change simply requires reinterpretation and a reevaluation of our expectations. Most often the desire to abandon our jobs or relationships stem from a sense of no longer feeling empowered. In these moments we are being presented with an opportunity to examine these power drains; where, when and to whom have we surrendered our power. When we fail to make these assessments we run the risk of repeating these experiences. It is important to remember that we don't lose or fail at life and that all choices are valid in the moment. We do however have the opportunity to select different experiences. Letting go of personal or external blame is much like cleaning your computer's hard drive; a disk cleanup removes unnecessary files. This in turn frees up more space allowing the computer to be more efficient and run more quickly in processing data at increased speed.

This is not about the outdated overhyped prosperity and abundance messages, enough already. This kind of mindset serves to reinforce a sense of lack. We then see prosperity as something out there that we have to journey to. Money is indeed a catalyst and presents us with many opportunities to experience many forms of lack in our reality which we associate with cash flow. The fact is that money flows in our lives according to the experiences and beliefs that we are still attached to and appear to still be engaged in. This swings to both sides of the pendulum from plenty to lack. When we are able to recognize the stories before us reality more easily and quickly shifts but will always shift according to each new version of your story/s. Reality is about a mindset which further determines our experiences along the path of time. This we call the journey. The fact is that the journey represents our traverse from one belief to the next. There really is no "time" or "distance" being measured only the switching of beliefs which presents us with our perspectives.

I remember experiencing this strong sense of comfort in receiving a regular paycheck. This level of comfort made me uncomfortable. To some this sounds a bit crazy but I was well aware of the trappings of this kind of experience. I didn't want to become drawn into the illusion of security, and I understood just how easy it was to be pulled in by the tide of comfort and security. These were just my own personal hang-ups, particularly in ensuring that I didn't give my power away to these external forces. My opposition to being controlled had at times launched me into a few interesting choices and experiences. These were all things that I needed to change and the corporate world eventually made clear to me that it was only responding to my beliefs! They did not control me but rather presented me with conditions that would appear as if I was being controlled.

I look back and I am forever grateful for the expansion that came from these experiences. To become aware that we are caught in the limitations of our comfortable and safe life can be ground breaking. It's very easy not to notice being stuck or even why you are stuck.

This is an opportunity to examine the payoffs in your stories, in the life that you are experiencing. Examine your areas of focus and investment and perhaps choose to reengage with self-empowerment, self-reliance and rise up in resilience! These were all the reasons why I created this Simple Ways to Step Outside of Your Comfort Zone 7 Day Program. May you be empowered by this 7 day course as you chart a new adventure and let go of an outdated life!

Simple ways to step outside of your comfort zone!

Letting go of an outdated life

Welcome to this 7 Day Course/Program

One of the first things to assert is that you are in charge of where you go from here. The question is where is it that you "think" you want to go. This leads to an introspective on how you are actually interpreting your life. There is generally a deep feeling of lack in making spiritual leaps (what we define as spiritual). Much of these conclusions are a result of measuring one's self to a thought, a belief, another individual or spiritual programming. What are those tools of measurement being used? It's time to take notice of these patterns which you have been operating by. This 7 Day Program is an opportunity for you to become more present in your life instead of the general automated habits and patterns. These old automated behaviors' creates challenges in maintaining consistency when attempting to integrate new experiences. Your interpretation of why you can't seem to break through this ceiling becomes a mystery and a focus; whereby solidifying the experience into a looping pattern. This will generally be interpreted as "being stuck"!

What you will be working with:

- There are a total of 14 guidance systems, 1 for each day, one in the morning and 1 in the evening for 7 days.

- Be sure to take a picture of yourself before starting this course. We change from moment to moment and as certain changes take place within us we are affected outwards as well.

- This book provides you with the daily steps and a few additional tips

- In the back of the book are forms allowing you to document your response to your daily experiences (use pencil)

- It's ok to repeat the steps in Day 1 until you feel ready to move forward. Please realize that this is about you being present in the moment and listening and feeling a true connection and completion of each step.

- It may take you two weeks to complete the 7 days but that's what it's about. Don't race through it but at the same time don't drag your feet. Repeat each day as necessary according to what is felt after certain steps have been experienced.

- This is about stepping beyond regret and self-blame but instead focusing on the steps necessary for moving beyond a static sort of life.

- It is about your commitment to letting go and to being open. You are authorizing your brain and your mind to remove the limiting filters

- Allow yourself to see!

- Know that you will see!

- Step beyond your expectations of the usual patterns of thoughts telling you that you can't break through.

- You are hacking and reprogramming yourself (your automated self)!

Are you stuck in a comfort zone? How to spot it!

Explore the following questions and observe your response

- Are you free to explore your ideas Yes __ No __
- Do you always have a reason why you "cant" explore your ideas/dreams Yes __ No __
- Are you convinced that the demands of life is holding you back Yes __ No __
- Do you believe that your relationship is holding you back Yes __ No __
- Do you cling to security Yes __ No __
- Do you tell yourself that once you obtain the ideal amount of money only then will take a chance Yes __ No __
- Are you ever able to hold on to that ideal amount of money
  Yes __ No __
- Do you work at being a good person, a nice person, a liked person Yes __ No __
- Do you "try" to remain positive Yes __ No __

- Do you have a disdain for so called "negative" people
  Yes __ No __
- Do you believe that negative people bring you down Yes __ No __
- How panicked are you if you don't have a health care plan or 401k, or some sort of retirement plan Yes __ No __
- Are you content with simply paying your bills Yes __ No __
- Do you blame your age as a factor in seeking or not seeking to do more Yes __ No __
- Are you able to set your watch by your daily routine Yes __ No __

Change is Entirely Up to You!

Transformation

Day 1

DAY 1 – Morning

1. What is this evolutionary leap you envision or yearn for…what does it look like in your mind?
2. What do you hold in your comfort zone; what are your fears about leaving your predictable behavior
3. Allow yourself to see the interpretation or conclusions you've drawn about your life
4. Clarify for yourself this lack you feel in yearning for more expansive levels of consciousness/awareness or life in general
5. What tools are you using to draw comparisons or what are the gages used in measuring your growth causing you to arrive at these conclusions in your mind?
6. Once you have written your answers to these questions, go about your day with an awareness of these questions along with the answers you expressed.
7. Truly observe your moment to moment function. This is your blueprint at work. Be sure to jot down observations that seem to have significant influence in the manner in which you have interpreted your life

DAY 1 – Evening

1. Your work day is now over or the most mentally demanding part of your day has ended. What is your general feeling; tired, weary, exhilarated?.... In one word what is the overall feeling. Do not over analyze it but rather grab the first obvious thought that comes to mind

2. What activities are you drawn to when you end your day (don't change it just observe for now)

3. What are the things or projects you find yourself putting off

4. What excuses do you notice entering your thoughts in postponing your movement towards these desires

5. How much of your focus is centered on the requirements of the game/reality such as bills or obligations

6. If you do engage in a meditation practice before bed take an honest assessment of what feeling/s you are left with when completed. Is it just a ritual or is there deep satisfaction at the end

7. Observe your thought process once in bed, what are you randomly thinking about
8. Are there sound or light distractions in the bedroom
9. How easily do you enter the sleep state

Day 2

DAY 2 – Morning

1. What are the first series of thoughts streaming in upon waking in the morning
2. How much of the dream world do you remember?
3. What's your first criticism of yourself for the day (what's your first judgment in first seeing your face in the mirror for the day)
4. Does the day feel like a rewind; just a repeat of every day prior
5. Make a decision on one activity or behavior that you will do differently today
6. Repeat Day 1 Steps 1-7 in addition
   a. What is this evolutionary leap that you envision or yearn for…what does it look like in your mind? It's now time to zone in on the answers you wrote done yesterday
   b. What do you hold in your comfort zone; what are your fears about leaving your predictable behavior – process the answers you wrote down yesterday, what in your life validates these fears. NOW write an outline of what this story would look like if these fears were not in

your mind. In other words write a new story on paper and in this story those fears do not exist as a possibility, what would that life look like. Feel it, give it texture!

c. Allow yourself to see the interpretation or conclusions you've drawn about your life (Identify anything in your reality that affirms this interpretation in your mind, write them down and determine exactly in what way is this interference occurring – a truthful examination)

d. Clarify this lack you feel as you yearn for more expansive levels of consciousness/awareness or of life in general – take a look at the previous answers yesterday, of what you believe is missing, what is this lack you feel. What is this lack made of, what in your reality validates this lack. Be in deeper observance today of this lack. Are there specific moments when this feeling arises more strongly (what's going on in your life when it does) On closer examination does the desire seem to be more a sense of wanting to

ESCAPE! If so, what are you escaping?

e. What models are used in measuring (making comparison) your growth bringing you to these conclusions in your mind? Really examine what this growth "should" in your mind look like

f. Once you have written your answers to these questions, go about your day with an awareness of these questions and the answers you expressed.

g. Truly observe your moment to moment function. Be sure to jot down observations that seem have significant influence in the manner that you have interpreted your life

7. Be present (means to be in the moment of what's occurring, don't travel into the past or into the future)

DAY 2 – Evening

1. End of the thinking part of the day – either do something different after leaving work before heading home. This could be the slightest of changes. It could simply be a different thought other than what's for dinner and of the things that you will routinely do once you are home. Perhaps even observing the people and traffic differently as characters in a play and your role in that play. Recognize your own performance

2. Do something different on arriving home – if you have a family at home perhaps see them differently, see them from a level of gratitude for being in your story. If you live alone see the beauty in your being with yourself at this time. Allow yourself to see more deeply into the gift of your present status of living alone. Why did you create this moment in time in this manner? What are the deeper opportunities being presented to you? Affirm that "I am ready to take life to the next level. I give my permission and I am open". Settle into that knowing and that feeling

3. While in bed focus on thoughts of awakening in a different version of reality. Close your eyes and really drink in that feeling. Drink in the truth that this is possible. Let it saturate your whole being (focus on the feeling – don't focus on what you don't want or what you don't have)

4. Prepare to get out of bed the next morning knowing that this day is new

Day 3

DAY 3 – Morning

When you woke up were you able to reaffirm that the day is new? If so how did you feel coming out of the sleep state

Let me be clear as you will repeat this process every morning:

a. When you awake immediately tune into to your sense of emerging from the state of sleep, you are training yourself to notice your return to this life and to notice the download of thoughts streaming in.

b. If you immediately notice that even for a brief moment you have forgotten about all of your usual worry, concerns and beliefs...then do your best to hang on to that feeling. When this happens it means that your day can be a different reality unless you begin to incorporate the usual thought process. It's very common for us to remind ourselves about the things that we were worried about yesterday or for the past months or years. The same with being sick, for a brief moment you may notice that on waking you forget that you aren't well but you quickly reaffirm that you are sick and it all comes flooding back. This is the manner in which we become caught in a loop and continue to run the same life every day. It requires that we activate the programs and the beliefs.

c. This is now an opportunity to incorporate sensations of what you wish to experience in your day. It is an opportunity to write your script for the day. You can say things like "today is an amazingly powerful day for me" or "today all dilemmas have been resolved" "today I will experience magic" and perhaps you don't have a specific instruction or thought but simply a sense of wellbeing...then go with that feeling. Once you determine the story for the day your only focus should be that thought or feeling. No looking back to the past or into the future

d. This is about nailing the NOW moment that you tapped into and staying there all day.

e. Understand that your brain has shifted to a different realm and it is the realm that you stepped into in the NOW, you awoke in.

f. Observe the reality around you from that space without reverting back to the old programs/old actions and thoughts

g. You are stepping outside of your comfort zone

h. And lastly be reminded that to say that something isn't real is to assert that "something" is not in your field of focus; it is not your realm of focus. Remember that what is defined as "real" is that which has been crystalized. A thought form is crystalized and takes shape or form when our attention is directed towards it, our energy and emotions breathe life into that "realm" of focus. Hence what's "real" for us is then born, it is then before us and all around us.

i. With this realization you will see the importance of staying with the focus you zoned in on in the morning. You can also see why your life continues to be a repeat of the same patterns. You initiate the same programs daily. Have an amazing day and see you this evening!

DAY 3 – Evening

1. It is now the end of your active day. Continue to be in this new reality space.
2. Allow yourself to break end of day routines and follow any feelings that suggest something different
3. Take notice of any push back against breaking your usual protocols, if so how did you feel stepping outside of normal habits
4. What have you been saying that you would like to do either at the end of the day or after work, at home or away from home
5. List at least 3 new habits that you would like to incorporate at the end of the day or during the day
6. Recognize behavior that perhaps affects your health/body such as food, which you habitually indulge in despite knowing the outcome
7. If so why do you believe that is? Speak to yourself and get answers
8. Determine if you are satisfied with the way you carried out the steps from this morning
9. If you are not satisfied, determine what it is that you aren't satisfied with

10. Did you struggle with old habits overriding your effort

11. Did you have feelings that dictated that you couldn't do this

12. Before going to bed get a solid sense of the outcome of the day

13. Determine how you would like to feel tomorrow, if you loved the way that you felt today then aim for it tomorrow

14. Once in bed zone in on creating a new reality and feel those feelings as you go off to sleep. Notice any push back from your mind in wanting to focus on problems or other issues. This is important because you are taking all of this into the dream state and waking up ready to repeat the same reality again. You begin creating the loop before entering asleep.

Have an amazing time creating your next moment. See you in the morning!

Day 4

DAY 4 –Morning

1. Repeat the steps from DAY 3's morning
2. Today lay in bed and turn that focus into a meditation
3. This meditation is about feeling this NOW moment through your entire body
4. Lay flat on your back, eyes closed and fully embody the moment
5. Realize and become saturated in knowing that the only thing that is real and true for me right now is this moment and that every future concern is only a speculation
6. Feel that you are different, drink it in, feel that your environment is different
7. Remind yourself that "real" is realm of focus, what's real for you right now, where is your focus?
8. Do this every morning for about 5 minutes, let this become a habit, establish the rules for your day with conviction
9. Now shift your focus a bit and say to yourself that "life is a game, now how do I choose to play it" "life doesn't play me, I play life". I am the writer, the game designer and the story teller.

10. Once you have drummed this in with conviction then you are ready to get out the bed

11. Know that when you step out of the bed you are stepping into the new reality you created

12. What's your first assessment of your reflection in the mirror?

13. This new reality that you have asserted should follow through all the way to the mirror, how do you see yourself or judge yourself

14. Be sure to see your projects as being done with ease for the day

15. Does this all mean that you will never have an off day? No! However this is an exercise that will pull you out of that space very quickly whereas before you may find yourself spiraling out of control in dealing with many adverse circumstances

16. If throughout the course of the day, challenges appear, old familiar, take a truthful observation of the attention you willingly give to these old habits

17. Is there fear that if they aren't there then you won't know what to do?

18. These habits and the feelings invested in them require your power. Who are you still trying to save? What is your dialog and

relationship like with the players in these habits

19. Go about your day with all of these steps of awareness

20. This will all become part of you

DAY 4 Evening

1. It's the end of the thinking period of the day again. Follow steps from DAY 3 evening.
2. Have you began to incorporate the 3 new habits that you would like to incorporate at the end of the day or during the day
3. If you haven't yet done so, implement the necessary steps for creating these three new habits
4. If the implementation of these new habits require that you wait for someone else in order to move forward then it may be necessary to explore steps to move forward on your own
5. Most often waiting on others to carry out a plan becomes just another excuse, it's a way to delay action. Generally moving forward on your own might get the ball rolling with the other party
6. Are you afraid to go it alone? Is it fear of taking chances
7. What is it that you fear about launching into these ideas on your own
8. Were you able to acknowledge behavior that perhaps affect your health/body such

as food ; things that you habitually indulge in despite knowing the outcome

9. What steps are you taking towards creating these changes

10. Are you now able to notice just how predictable your life might be at this time?

11. Tonight begin to list three projects or less that you have had a strong desire to build

12. Underneath each project list what it is that you fear about starting the project

13. I want you to go to bed with this on your mind, let these ideas swirl around your mind before sleeping. Feel the excitement about the prospect of these projects existing

14. What do they look and feel like as you lay in bed. Feel them as if they already exist

15. Do not focus on what you DON'T have in order to bring this project to life. Instead focus on what they feel like in existence.

16. Dream yourself into the realm of possibility where it already exists

17. Take note of the dream state

18. Take note of your thoughts on coming out of the sleep state

19. Plan to awake in an even more expansive reality

Wishing you an awesome night of dreaming, see you in the morning!

Day 5

DAY 5 –Morning

1. Repeat DAY 4 morning
2. Before going to bed you had to list three projects and enter the sleep state feeling these ideas and excitement about them
3. What did you feel last night in doing this exercise
4. Were they in your memory on waking this morning
5. How did you feel coming out of sleep this morning was it different from yesterday and if so what was different about it
6. Before getting out of bed laying on your back in this form of meditative focus, feel the possibility of at least one of these project being initiated
7. Today begin to list the necessary steps to set this/these projects in motion
8. Begin to do research, document notes, phone numbers and contacts. Use the worksheet as a guideline
9. Is there any pushback from your mind about this, old habits popping through
10. Projects can be anything from writing an article, taking a trip to building a house, its

anything that has become an out of reach dream

11. Sometimes it's best to work with yourself before sharing with others.

12. Know who those parties are that will test your confidence and resilience, e.g. if you share this with someone knowing that they will not be supportive then you have opened yourself up to doubt. However this is more than likely what is needed should you elect to do so in knowing the nature of this character. It may also be a way to sabotage yourself into shutting down your efforts.

13. Go about your day observing yourself as you create this new you and incorporating new possibilities

Have a splendid day dream, see you this evening!

DAY 5 –Evening

1. The end of another day!
2. Review and repeat Day 4 evening as appropriate
3. How are those three new habits coming along, be it working out, a change of diet, not dropping your shoes off in the middle of the floor, placing your keys where you can find them, working smarter not harder? Whatever it maybe have you began!
4. Remember that you are building habits that you can continue to build on. You are learning to consciously retrain your brain to a new blueprint
5. You are creating a new blueprint for your brain to follow. Repetition begins to build into a normal way of operating. This is the formula for everything that you wish to experience.
6. How do you break into other realms of possibilities if you cannot break through the ceiling of your everyday illusion? You begin the process with these very simple steps
7. So far what are the results of bringing your project/s to life
8. Are you satisfied with your research?

9. Can you see yourself starting this project?

10. Perhaps select one of your projects that can be started at any time

11. When do you see yourself testing the waters and starting if nothing else the planning of it. Is there a place that you have wanted to visit, what will it take for you to get there. Plan it. Once you begin the process of planning the very idea begin to open up opportunities. These opportunities exist but you must initiate the possibility so that you may step into that field

12. Are you scared? If so why? What does this mean for you?

13. Have you continued to do something different each day?

14. Take these dreams into the dream world not as a worry or concern but as a dream that you are crystalizing into form. Always feel it as if it already exists.

15. Plan to wake into a reality that supports these dreams

Have another amazing dream adventure and see you in the morning!

Day 6

DAY 6 – Morning

1. Repeat previous morning steps
   a. Pay attention to download of first thoughts streaming
   b. Reaffirm that today is new, a new reality
   c. Affirming mediation on your back
2. Take note of dreams that standout in your mind on waking
3. Is there anything that stands out while going off to sleep with your projects in mind
4. Since processing the steps from day 1 - 5 are there still situations and conditions in your life which remain a concern for you, a worry perhaps
   a. What steps are available to you in moving beyond these concerns
   b. If so what are the reasons you've presented yourself for not taking those steps
   c. Are your reasons valid
   d. What are the patterns that you have created around these situations

    e. Could the implementation of any of these projects be a solution to your concerns

    f. What has been the payoff of these conditions? There is always a payoff – it's important to acknowledge them as they have become part of your normal. They support the ongoing nature of your concerns. What do they afford you? Are you ready to let go of the payoffs? Payoffs can be anything from attention to excuses to avoid leaving your comfort zone to partnership/companionship, a topic of discussion, a point of focus, something to always concern yourself with etc.

5. Add this to your focus today, go through these questions and answer them honestly.

6. Then incorporate the relevant steps from all that you have been doing

7. This is not just about a series of steps but about you establishing your own tools from these steps. You are acquiring the necessary skills to pull yourself out of any situation.

8. Remember that where your attention is focused becomes the "realm" in which you will operate it. It becomes your reality and

in so doing stores and characters are built in to support the payoff. You must be willing and ready to give up the payoff

9. It's time to fill that space with new activities, new possibilities

10. This includes relationships and partnerships that are stagnating but have become comfort zones. One may imagine being outside of a stagnating, suffocating and limiting relationship but yet scared to leave the safety of this predictable space. This is a fear of leaving ones comfort zone.

11. If this is your situation then examine all the reasons you've given yourself about your acceptance of it. Take those reasons apart.

    a. You will perhaps need to spend a few days processing this step

    b. Begin to allow yourself to feel what it would feel like living a different experiences, one that is lighter and free

    c. If you cannot step away then begin to plan a life filled with activities and opportunities that bring you joy, such as beginning that long held project

    d. When you give yourself permission to live and you begin to take the necessary steps towards living, then your life will begin to shift

12. Have an amazing day of discovery! See you this evening!

DAY 6 – Evening

It's the evening of Day 6

1. You have had a lot to process today, What is your state of mind after the days process
2. Take the evening to review the areas of focus from this morning's steps
3. It is perfectly fine to step away to take a break if need be and repeat day 6 tomorrow
4. The idea is to pin point the areas in your life that your comfort zone is tied to or is the root of your comfort zone
5. Now that you have been made aware of many of your thoughts, beliefs and actions that simply repeat themselves as a pattern, allow yourself to see the limitations as they pop up, it's not just about feeing good but it is about you lightening your load of limiting beliefs.

Day 7

Day 7 - Morning

1. Repeat the previous steps
    a. Being aware of the download of thoughts
    b. Remind yourself that today is new, a new reality
    c. Move into your meditative focus before getting out of bed
    d. Create the day (as in previous steps)
    e. Tune into the results of the past 6 days

GOING ABOUT YOUR DAY

Take as much time as needed to focus on any of the following steps that require deep thought.

2. This being day 7 have you noticed any new changes in your life and in your behavior
3. Have you been forming new habits
4. Is there still tension in taking these steps forward
5. If there is tension then determine why
6. Today examine and address your spiritual beliefs, are you in a spiritual comfort zone
7. Can you truthfully identify spiritual beliefs holding you immobile

8. If so why, what is it about that/those belief/s that cause you to cling to it
9. Today is the day to surrender to inner freedom, give yourself permission to let go
10. Realize that the limitations that you cling to are concepts, ideas, rules and protocols based on someone else's design
11. Let go of your fear of failure
12. Let go of your fear of disappointing others
13. Say to yourself "I let go of old stories and old patterns that no longer serve me" "I give myself permission to change the story"
14. Let go of your guilt and shame (this is all an illusion)
15. Step into your day and out into the game knowing that you are different, knowing that while everything around you may appear the same, you are in a different reality

Have an amazing day of truth and affirmations! I will see you this evening!

Day 7 Evening

1. It is the end of your day.
2. What are the results from the morning's steps?
3. Do you feel a need to repeat this 7 day program? I recommend you repeat it as often as needed throughout the course of life in general
4. Take a deep breath, relax and do what you feel
5. Perhaps take yourself to dinner or a movie or even a quite bath with all the trimming, candles, incense, music, a glass of wine, in honor of the changes you have been making
6. Treat yourself like the best friend that you are to yourself
7. Say no to stressful obligations this evening
8. It's all about you
9. Let go of any leftover guilt or shame, be reminded that "those were just experiences"
10. Repeat the steps for bed or go to any page you wish for a brief reminder

Sleep amazingly well as tomorrow is a brand new reality and a brand new version of the character you play!

DAY 1 - RESPONSE MORNING

Date _____

_____

_____

_____

_____

_____

_____

_____

_____

_____

_____

_____

_____

_____

_____

_____

_____

_____

_____

_____

_____

_____

_____

_____

_____

Simple ways to step outside of your comfort zone

_____
_____
_____
_____
_____
_____
_____
_____
_____
_____
_____
_____
_____
_____
_____
_____
_____
_____
_____
_____
_____
_____
_____
_____
_____
_____
_____
_____

Simple ways to step outside of your comfort zone

_____

_____

_____

_____

_____

_____

_____

_____

_____

_____

_____

_____

_____

_____

_____

_____

_____

_____

_____

_____

_____

_____

_____

_____

_____

_____

_____

_____

_____

DAY 1 - RESPONSE EVENING

Date _____

_____

_____

_____

_____

_____

_____

_____

_____

_____

_____

_____

_____

_____

_____

_____

_____

_____

_____

_____

_____

_____

_____

_____

Simple ways to step outside of your comfort zone

_____

_____

_____

_____

_____

_____

_____

_____

_____

_____

_____

_____

_____

_____

_____

_____

_____

_____

_____

_____

_____

_____

_____

_____

_____

_____

_____

_____

Simple ways to step outside of your comfort zone

DAY 2 - RESPONSE MORNING

Date _____

_____

_____

_____

_____

_____

_____

_____

_____

_____

_____

_____

_____

_____

_____

_____

_____

_____

_____

_____

_____

_____

_____

_____

_____

_____

Simple ways to step outside of your comfort zone

_____

_____

_____

_____

_____

_____

_____

_____

_____

_____

_____

_____

_____

_____

_____

_____

_____

_____

_____

_____

_____

_____

_____

_____

_____

_____

Simple ways to step outside of your comfort zone

DAY 2 – RESPONSE EVENING

Date _____

_____

_____

_____

_____

_____

_____

_____

_____

_____

_____

_____

_____

_____

_____

_____

_____

_____

_____

_____

_____

_____

_____

_____

_____

Simple ways to step outside of your comfort zone

Simple ways to step outside of your comfort zone

_____

_____

_____

_____

_____

_____

_____

_____

_____

_____

_____

_____

_____

_____

_____

_____

_____

_____

_____

_____

_____

_____

_____

_____

_____

DAY 3 – RESPONSE MORNING

Date _____

_____

_____

_____

_____

_____

_____

_____

_____

_____

_____

_____

_____

_____

_____

_____

_____

_____

_____

_____

_____

_____

_____

_____

_____

_____

_____

Simple ways to step outside of your comfort zone

Simple ways to step outside of your comfort zone

_____
_____
_____
_____
_____
_____
_____
_____
_____
_____
_____
_____
_____
_____
_____
_____
_____
_____
_____
_____
_____
_____
_____
_____
_____
_____

DAY 3 – RESPONSE EVENING

Date _____

_____

_____

_____

_____

_____

_____

_____

_____

_____

_____

_____

_____

_____

_____

_____

_____

_____

_____

_____

_____

_____

_____

_____

_____

_____

Simple ways to step outside of your comfort zone

Simple ways to step outside of your comfort zone

_____
_____
_____
_____
_____
_____
_____
_____
_____
_____
_____
_____
_____
_____
_____
_____
_____
_____
_____
_____
_____
_____
_____
_____
_____
_____
_____

DAY 4 – RESPONSE MORNING

Date _____

_____

_____

_____

_____

_____

_____

_____

_____

_____

_____

_____

_____

_____

_____

_____

_____

_____

_____

_____

_____

_____

_____

_____

_____

Simple ways to step outside of your comfort zone

Simple ways to step outside of your comfort zone

DAY 4 – RESPONSE EVENING

Date _____

_____

_____

_____

_____

_____

_____

_____

_____

_____

_____

_____

_____

_____

_____

_____

_____

_____

_____

_____

_____

_____

_____

_____

_____

Simple ways to step outside of your comfort zone

_____

_____

_____

_____

_____

_____

_____

_____

_____

_____

_____

_____

_____

_____

_____

_____

_____

_____

_____

_____

_____

_____

_____

_____

_____

Simple ways to step outside of your comfort zone

_____

_____

_____

_____

_____

_____

_____

_____

_____

_____

_____

_____

_____

_____

_____

_____

_____

_____

_____

_____

_____

_____

_____

DAY 5 – RESPONSE MORNING

Date _____

_____

_____

_____

_____

_____

_____

_____

_____

_____

_____

_____

_____

_____

_____

_____

_____

_____

_____

_____

_____

_____

_____

_____

_____

Simple ways to step outside of your comfort zone

Simple ways to step outside of your comfort zone

_____

_____

_____

_____

_____

_____

_____

_____

_____

_____

_____

_____

_____

_____

_____

_____

_____

_____

_____

_____

_____

_____

_____

DAY 5 – EVENING

Date _____

_____

_____

_____

_____

_____

_____

_____

_____

_____

_____

_____

_____

_____

_____

_____

_____

_____

_____

_____

_____

_____

_____

_____

Simple ways to step outside of your comfort zone

_____

_____

_____

_____

_____

_____

_____

_____

_____

_____

_____

_____

_____

_____

_____

_____

_____

_____

_____

_____

_____

_____

_____

_____

_____

Simple ways to step outside of your comfort zone

DAY 6 – RESPONSE MORNING

Date _____

_____

_____

_____

_____

_____

_____

_____

_____

_____

_____

_____

_____

_____

_____

_____

_____

_____

_____

_____

_____

_____

_____

_____

_____

_____

_____

Simple ways to step outside of your comfort zone

_____

_____

_____

_____

_____

_____

_____

_____

_____

_____

_____

_____

_____

_____

_____

_____

_____

_____

_____

_____

_____

_____

_____

_____

_____

_____

Simple ways to step outside of your comfort zone

_____
_____
_____
_____
_____
_____
_____
_____
_____
_____
_____
_____
_____
_____
_____
_____
_____
_____
_____
_____
_____
_____
_____
_____
_____

DAY 6 – RESPONSE EVENING

Date _____

_____

_____

_____

_____

_____

_____

_____

_____

_____

_____

_____

_____

_____

_____

_____

_____

_____

_____

_____

_____

_____

_____

_____

_____

_____

Simple ways to step outside of your comfort zone

_____
_____
_____
_____
_____
_____
_____
_____
_____
_____
_____
_____
_____
_____
_____
_____
_____
_____
_____
_____
_____
_____
_____
_____
_____
_____
_____

Simple ways to step outside of your comfort zone

_____

_____

_____

_____

_____

_____

_____

_____

_____

_____

_____

_____

_____

_____

_____

_____

_____

_____

_____

_____

_____

_____

_____

_____

DAY 7 – RESPONSE MORNING

Date _____

_____

_____

_____

_____

_____

_____

_____

_____

_____

_____

_____

_____

_____

_____

_____

_____

_____

_____

_____

_____

_____

_____

_____

_____

_____

Simple ways to step outside of your comfort zone

_____
_____
_____
_____
_____
_____
_____
_____
_____
_____
_____
_____
_____
_____
_____
_____
_____
_____
_____
_____
_____
_____
_____
_____
_____

Simple ways to step outside of your comfort zone

_____

_____

_____

_____

_____

_____

_____

_____

_____

_____

_____

_____

_____

_____

_____

_____

_____

_____

_____

_____

_____

_____

_____

DAY 7 – RESPONSE EVENING

Date _____

_____

_____

_____

_____

_____

_____

_____

_____

_____

_____

_____

_____

_____

_____

_____

_____

_____

_____

_____

_____

_____

_____

_____

Simple ways to step outside of your comfort zone

_____
_____
_____
_____
_____
_____
_____
_____
_____
_____
_____
_____
_____
_____
_____
_____
_____
_____
_____
_____
_____
_____
_____
_____
_____
_____
_____
_____

Simple ways to step outside of your comfort zone

_____

_____

_____

_____

_____

_____

_____

_____

_____

_____

_____

_____

_____

_____

_____

_____

_____

_____

_____

_____

_____

_____

_____

_____

_____

LIST YOUR THREE PROJECTS

➢ _____
_____
_____
_____
_____

➢ _____
_____
_____
_____
_____

➢ _____
_____
_____
_____
_____

NOTES

_____
_____
_____
_____
_____

Simple ways to step outside of your comfort zone

_____
_____
_____
_____
_____
_____
_____
_____
_____
_____
_____
_____

STEPS TO BEGIN YOUR FIRST PROJECT

Step 1. Name of your first project

_____

_____

Step 2. List the requirements to begin

_____

_____

_____

_____

_____

_____

_____

_____

Step 3. List where you will begin your research

_____

_____

_____

_____

_____

_____

_____

_____

Step 4. Document the results of that research

_____

_____

_____

_____

_____

_____

_____

_____

_____

_____

Step 5. Follow through!

Step 6. Be excited about the possibility!

Step 7. Stay present in building that dream – build it in your mind as you proceed

Step 8. What do you observe about yourself as you proceed – what is your thinking like, such as potential bombarding thoughts

_____

_____

_____

_____

_____

_____

_____

_____

Step 9. What steps are you taking to override those fears?

_____

_____

_____

_____

_____

_____

_____

_____

Step 10. Be consistent and stay with the story you are creating

_____

_____

_____

Simple ways to step outside of your comfort zone

_____

_____

_____

_____

Basic steps to change

- Being present
- Commit to change
- Commit to yourself
- Stop the over analysis
- Reevaluate those things you identify as important
- Overwhelm – what experiences are defining your state of overwhelm?
- Establish a habit/a pattern of operating
- Continue to stretch those habits by adding to them/make those changes evolutionary – so that you will never be stuck/static

Daily practices before getting out of bed

- Observe your thoughts on waking
- Focus on being present
- Affirm that today is new – a different reality
- Remind yourself that "all that exists is this moment"(this deters you from running the same programs as a loop)
- Allow your entire being to be part of this focus
- Acknowledge your body as well (thank your joints, organs, cells etc.)
- Set your day before getting out of bed – what kind of day would you like to experience?
- Decide to do something different and new today (you can be spontaneous, so this doesn't not have to be preplanned)
- When you are done get out of bed knowing that when you step out of bed you step into the reality you created for the day

Daily practices before sleep

- Review the events of the day before getting in bed
- Decide what changes you would like to make
- While in bed remind yourself that tomorrow is a new reality and that you can make it completely different from today
- Be present - meaning not to speculate in worry about the future – remind yourself that "the only thing that exist is the moment, everything else is speculative"
- Any challenges you faced today realize that you do not have to bring that story along into tomorrow. "Reality is pliable, it is in constant flux" However it will keep replaying the patterns that are a consistent focus for you
- Bring those changes along into your sleep/dream state

Sleep well and dream well!

THOUGHT PROVOKING QUOTES

"My life is not defined by corporations, government or systems of power, but by my own knowledge and choices"

Sonia Barrett

"Anyone who has never made a mistake has never tried anything new."

Albert Einstein

"I would say that in my scientific and philosophical work, my main concern has been with understanding the nature of reality in general and of consciousness in particular as a coherent whole, which is never static or complete but which is an unending process of movement and unfoldment...."

D. Bohm, _Wholeness and the Implicate Order

"Change is entirely up to you"

Sonia Barrett

"Two things are infinite: the universe and human stupidity; and I'm not sure about the universe."

Albert Einstein

"The ability to perceive or think differently is more important than the knowledge gained. "

David Bohm

"My suggestion is that at each state the proper order of operation of the mind requires an overall grasp of what is generally known, not only in formal logical, mathematical terms, but also intuitively, in images, feelings, poetic usage of language, etc."

David Bohm

"Life is like riding a bicycle. To keep your balance, you must keep moving."

Albert Einstein
"Lay a firm foundation with the bricks that others throw at you."

David Brinkley

"The greatest mistake you can make in life is to continually fear you will make one."

Elbert Hubbard

"You are the fabric from which your reality is created, what's woven into this fabric?"

Sonia Barrett

IN CONCLUSION

Now that you have come to the end of this handbook I'd like to remind you that this moment in time is presenting you with an opportunity to examine the payoffs in your stories; in the life that you are experiencing.

To examine where we place importance identifies where much of our creative energy is placed. Those things of importance require focused attention. Examine your degree of focus and investment and rise up in resilience! May you be empowered by this 7 day series of insights and practical steps. The journey isn't out there somewhere, you are the journey!

The Beginning!

TO ORDER THE VIDEO AND AUDIO VERSION

OF THIS 7 DAY PROGRAM

VISIT

www.therealsoniabarrett.com

(Additional books and products by Sonia Barrett
also available on the website)

Simple ways to step outside of your comfort zone

Simple ways to step outside of your comfort zone